D1265735

LIGHTNING BOLT BOOKS™

The Energy We See

A Look at Light

Jennifer Boothroyd

Lerner Publications Company

Minneapolis

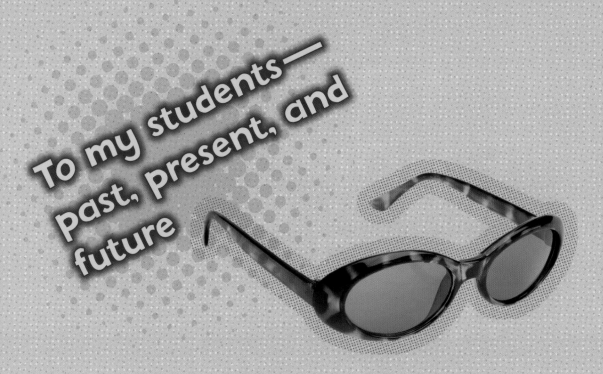

To my students—
past, present, and
future

Lerner Publications Company
A division of Lerner Publishing Group, Inc.
241 First Avenue North
Minneapolis, MN 55401 U.S.A.

Website address: www.lernerbooks.com

Library of Congress Cataloging-in-Publication Data

Boothroyd, Jennifer, 1972–
    The energy we see: a look at light / by Jennifer Boothroyd.
        p.   cm. — (Lightning bolt books™ — Exploring physical science)
    Includes index.
    ISBN 978–0–7613–6092–6 (lib. bdg. : alk. paper)
        1. Light—Juvenile literature. I. Title.
    QC360.B645 2011
    535—dc22   2010004743

Manufactured in the United States of America
1 — CG — 12/31/10

Contents

What Is Light?

Light is a form of energy. It is an important part of life on this planet.

Light helps plants grow.

Most of the light on Earth
comes from the sun. The sun
is a natural source of light.

Fireflies and lightning are also natural sources of light. Fire gives off natural light as well.

This campfire is a natural light source.

People have created ways to produce light. This is called artificial light.

Jacob's reading lamp gives off artificial light.

Long ago, people used candles or oil lamps for light.

A young man reads by candlelight in the 1600s.

These days, electricity is mostly used to create light.

Lightbulbs, flashlights, and TV screens give off light.

How Light Travels

Light energy travels in waves. Light waves move in straight lines until they hit an object.

Nothing moves faster than light. Light from the sun takes only eight minutes to reach Earth.

The light bounces off the object. This is called reflection.

Light waves move like Ping-Pong balls. They bounce off objects and keep moving.

All objects reflect light. We are able to see things because the light bounces off the object and back to our eyes.

Light bounces off this book.

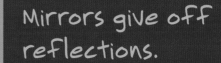

Mirrors give off reflections.

Smooth and shiny objects reflect light well. Objects that reflect light well give off reflections. Reflections let us see what is nearby.

Light Stops Here

Some objects are made from opaque materials. Opaque materials stop light waves from moving through them.

Louis can't see through this opaque blindfold.

Shine a small flashlight toward the wall in a dark room. Then cover the lit end of the flashlight with a book. The light will no longer shine on the wall. The opaque book will block the light.

Next hold a pencil in front of the lit end of the flashlight. You'll see a dark area on the wall in the shape of the pencil. This is the pencil's shadow.

When an object blocks light, it makes a shadow. Bigger objects make bigger shadows. Smaller objects make smaller shadows.

The shadow of a large tree provides shade on a hot day.

17

Just Passing Through

Other objects are made from transparent materials. Transparent materials let light pass through them. Glass is a transparent material.

We can see clearly through a glass window.

Put a piece of clear plastic wrap over the flashlight.

Point the flashlight at a wall once again. Light moves all the way through the transparent plastic wrap.

Translucent materials let only some light pass through. We can't see clearly through them. This lampshade is translucent.

only some of the light from this lightbulb shines through the lampshade.

The speed of a light wave changes when it passes through some materials. This change makes the light bend, or refract. Bent light can play tricks on our eyes.

Water in this stream refracts light. The fish are to the side of where we see them.

Look at the spoon in this glass of water. The handle looks broken because the water refracts the light.

The spoon is still in one piece.

Colors

The light we see looks white. But it is actually a mix of seven colors.

When light
is bent, you
can see the
different
colors. Red,
orange,
yellow, green,
blue, indigo,
and violet
create white
light together.

24

Light lets us see the color of an object. Try getting dressed in the dark. Can you tell the difference between your black and brown shoes?

Or your blue and gray socks?

We can see an object's color because the object only reflects light of that color back to our eyes. The other colors do not bounce off the object.

Green grass reflects green light waves. The red ball reflects red light waves.

The world would be a very boring place without light.

Activity
Indoor Rainbow

You can make a rainbow of your own!
Give this fun experiment a try.

What you need:

a white wall or a
dry-erase board

an old CD (ask an
adult to help
you find one)

a flashlight

What you do:

1. Stand near the white wall or dry-erase board in a dark room.

2. Hold the **CD** so the blank side faces the wall. Shine the flashlight toward the blank side of the **CD**. Tip the **CD** until you can see the rainbow colors on the wall.

What's going on? The tiny ridges on the **CD** are bending the light and splitting it into many colors.

Do you want to make more rainbows? Make a mobile by tying a bunch of **CD**s to a hanger with string. Hang the hanger near a sunny window. Watch the rainbows flash around the room.

Glossary

artificial: not natural, or made by people

electricity: a form of energy used to run motors and produce light

energy: a form of power that makes machines work and produces heat

natural: found in nature and not made by people

opaque: not letting light through

reflect: to bounce back

refract: to bend

shadow: a dark area made by an object blocking light waves

translucent: allowing some light to pass through

transparent: allowing all light to pass through

wave: a vibration of energy that travels through air or water

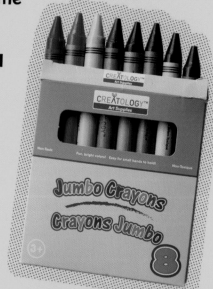

Further Reading

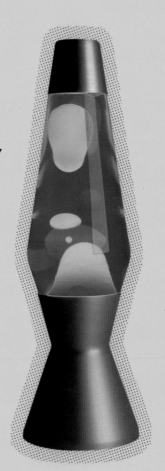

Dragonfly TV: Light and Color
http://pbskids.org/dragonflytv/
show/lightandcolor.html

Dussling, Jennifer. *The Rainbow Mystery*. Minneapolis: Kane Press, 2002.

The NASA Sci-Files: Light and Color
http://scifiles.larc.nasa.gov/
text/kids/Problem_Board/
problems/light/sim1.html

Physics4Kids: Light and Optics
http://www.physics4kids.com/
files/light_intro.html

Pipe, Jim. *Light: What Is a Shadow?* North Mankato, MN: Stargazer Books, 2006.

Walker, Sally M. *Light*. Lerner Publications Company, 2006.

Index

Photo Acknowledgments

The images in this book are used with the permission of: © iStockphoto.com/milosluz, p. 1; © D. Hurst/Alamy, p. 2; © iStockphoto.com/DNY59, p. 4; © Mike Grandmaison/CORBIS, p. 5; © Randy Faris/CORBIS, p. 6; © iStockphoto.com/Fransico Romero, p. 7; © Stomer/The Bridgeman Art Library/Getty Images, p. 8; © Chris Stein/Digital Vision/Getty Images, p. 9; NASA/NASA/ARC, p. 10; © RyuheShindo/Corbis Super RF/Alamy, p. 11; © Laura Westlund/Independent Picture Service, p. 12; © AZPworldwide/Shutterstock Images, p. 13; © Anyka/Shutterstock Images, p. 14; © kareem black/The Image Bank/Getty Images, p. 15; © Todd Strand/Independent Picture Service, p. 16; © Hummer/Digital Vision/Getty Images, p. 17; © Ben Molyneux People/Alamy, p. 18; © Karlene Schwartz, pp. 19, 30; © iStockphoto.com/Authur Fatykhov, p. 20; © Kevin Schafer/Peter Arnold, Inc./Alamy, p. 21; © iStockphoto.com/Louis Aguinaldo, p. 22; © Axel Fassio/Brand X Pictures/Getty Images, p. 23; © Ron Boardman/Life Science Image/Minden Pictures, p. 24; © vikky/Shutterstock Images, p. 25; © Image Source/Getty Images, p. 26; © Jim Cummins/Taxi/Getty Images, p. 27; © Alexstar/Dreamstime.com, p. 28 (CD); © Linqong/Dreamstime.com, p. 28 (Flashlight); © Paul Springett A/Alamy, p. 31.

Front cover: © Randy Faris/Corbis Premium RF/Alamy.